MOSES
Leader and Lawgiver

Retold by Jean Horton Berg
Original illustrations by Felix Palm

ISBN 978-0-87510-461-4

© 1982, 2008 The Christian Science Publishing Society
All rights reserved. Printed in the USA.

JMP0810005

Moses led the children of Israel out of bondage in Egypt to the land God promised them, and gave them the Ten Commandments.

This is his story. It's in the Bible, in the Old Testament.

Pharaoh, the ruler of Egypt, didn't like the Hebrews, the children of Israel. They weren't Egyptians, and he made them work very hard at tasks like making bricks by hand and building walls and roads.

He forgot that long before, another Pharaoh had invited them to live in Egypt because Joseph, a Hebrew, had saved the Egyptians during a terrible famine.

To keep their numbers from growing, Pharaoh ordered, "Throw every newborn Hebrew boy into the river!"

About that time a Hebrew woman bore a son. She hid him at home for three months. Then she wove a snug little ark of reeds and made it watertight with clay and tar. She laid her baby in the tiny basket and set it among the reeds by the water's edge.

Pharaoh's daughter came down to the river to bathe and saw the ark. She sent one of her maids to get it. "Oh," Pharaoh's daughter said softly when she opened it, "this is a Hebrew child."

The baby's sister, Miriam, who was nearby watching, ran up to her. "Shall I call a Hebrew woman to take care of the baby for you?" she asked.

When Pharaoh's daughter said yes, Miriam brought her own mother. So the baby lived with Miriam, his brother, Aaron, and his own parents.

When he was older, his mother took him to the king's palace to Pharaoh's daughter. She adopted him and named him Moses.

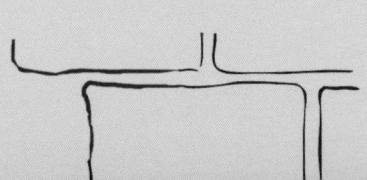

Although Moses grew up as an Egyptian prince, he never forgot that he was a Hebrew, one of the children of Israel. One day Moses saw an Egyptian boss beating a Hebrew worker. He was furious and killed the Egyptian.

The next day Moses saw two Hebrews fighting. "Why are you hitting your brother?" he asked the one who had started it.

"Who made you a judge over us?" the man snarled. "Will you kill me as you did that Egyptian?"

People knew what Moses had done! Pharaoh would have had him killed for this, so Moses fled from Egypt to the desert land of Midian.

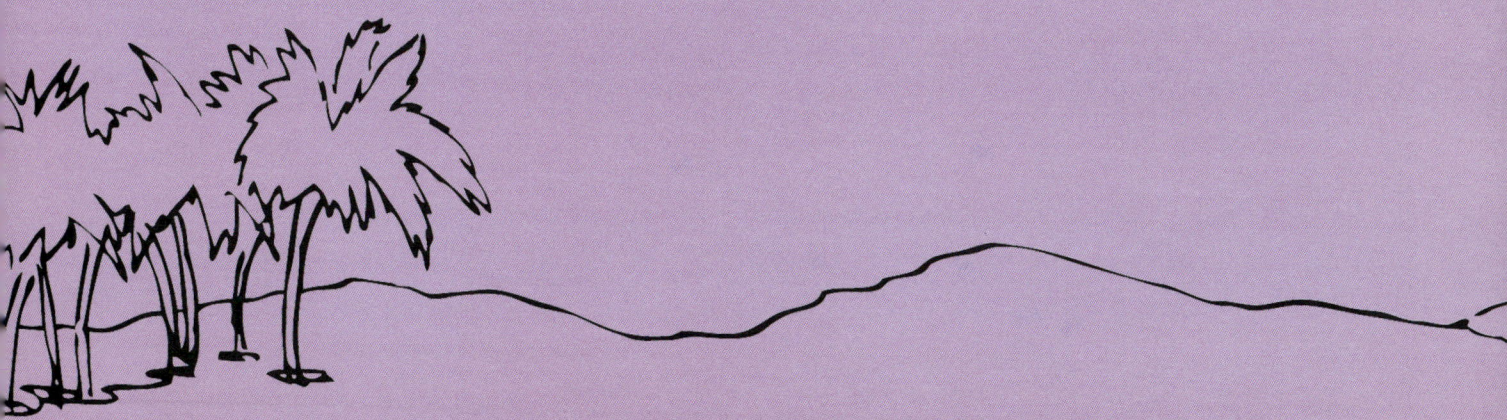

One day seven sisters drove their father's sheep to a well there to get water. As soon as they filled the troughs, some rough shepherds chased them away to take the water for their own animals. Moses saw what was happening and chased away the shepherds. Then he helped the young women water their sheep.

Moses married Zipporah, one of the sisters, and stayed in Midian. He became a shepherd, leading the sheep to find food and water, and watching over them.

One day he led the sheep across the desert to graze near Mount Sinai, which also had the name Mount Horeb. There he noticed a bush burning, but it never burned up! As he went over to see it better, a voice called, "Moses, Moses!"

"Here I am," Moses answered.

"I am the God of your fathers, the God of Abraham, the God of Isaac, and the God of Jacob," said the voice. "My people are having a hard time in Egypt. I'm going to bring them out of Egypt into a rich land flowing with milk and honey. I want you to lead them."

Moses was astonished. "Who am I to lead them?" he asked.

"Certainly I will be with you," God answered.

"They'll ask who sent me," Moses said anxiously. "They'll ask me Your name."

"Tell them I AM, the God of their fathers, sent you," God said.

"Well, they'll never believe me," Moses declared.

"What's that in your hand?" God asked.

"It's my shepherd's rod," Moses answered.

"Throw it on the ground," God told him.

The minute Moses threw down his rod, it became a snake. Moses ran from it.

"Now pick it up by the tail," God said.

As scary as this was, Moses did what God told him. The snake turned into a shepherd's rod again.

God gave Moses another sign of His power: He healed his hand which had suddenly become diseased.

"Show My people these signs," God said. "They will believe that God sent you."

"But I'm not a very good talker," Moses murmured.

"Well, who gives people speech?" God asked.
"Don't I? I'll tell you what to say."

Moses still held back. "Please send somebody else," he begged.

"Your brother, Aaron, speaks well," God said. "He'll go with you. I'll tell you what to say, and he'll say it for you. Take your shepherd's rod with you so that you can do signs that My people will believe."

So Moses went back to Egypt, and Aaron came out to meet him. They gathered together all the leaders of the children of Israel, and Aaron told them everything God had told Moses. Aaron showed the signs God had given, too. Then the children of Israel believed that God had sent Moses to lead them out of Egypt.

Now there was a new Pharaoh. When Moses and Aaron told him God wanted the Hebrews to leave Egypt, he roared, "I don't know any such God, and I won't let these people go!"

It wasn't until many bad things happened to the Egyptians that Pharaoh agreed to let the Hebrews go free.

They were hardly out of sight when he changed his mind. "Why ever did we let those workers go!" he cried.

Pharaoh chased the Hebrews with 600 chariots. He caught up with them at the Red Sea. God had led them there with a pillar of cloud by day, and a pillar of fire by night.

The Hebrews were terrified as the Egyptians rushed toward them. They cried out to God, and they said to Moses, "Why didn't you let us alone? We'd rather be slaves in Egypt than die here!"

"Don't be afraid," Moses said. "Stay right here, and see how God will take care of you. You'll never see the Egyptians again."

Then God told Moses to lift up his rod and stretch out his hand over the sea. Moses didn't ask why. He did what God said. All that night God made a strong east wind blow back the waters of the sea until the bottom was like dry land. The children of Israel walked easily across to the other side.

The Egyptians raced after them. But when they reached the middle of the sea, God told Moses to stretch out his hand again. Then the waters flowed back and covered the Egyptians.

The children of Israel were so happy that they sang a song of thanksgiving to God. "The Lord is my strength and song," they sang. "He is my deliverer."

Moses' sister, Miriam, took up a tambourine. The women followed her with tambourines and danced for joy while she sang, "Sing to the Lord, for He is victorious."

Now the people gladly followed Moses into the wilderness, until they got hungry!

"We should have stayed in Egypt," they howled. "At least we had enough to eat there. We'll die of hunger here!"

"They'll have plenty to eat," God promised Moses.

That night, flocks of quail flew into the camp. So there was meat. In the morning, tiny, round white things covered the ground. They tasted like wafers made with honey. The Hebrews said, "It is manna." Moses said, "God has given us bread."

Moses led his people on, knowing that God was caring for them. They had manna to eat, and water to drink; sometimes the water gushed out of bare rocks. But whenever anything went wrong, the Hebrews still doubted God and blamed Moses.

No matter what happened, Moses talked with God and did what God told him to do.

After many days in the wilderness, they came to Mount Sinai where Moses had seen the burning bush. They made camp at the foot of the mountain.

The children of Israel needed to understand not only their closeness to God, but also how to obey Him and how to get along with each other. So God called Moses to the top of Mount Sinai and said, "I am the Lord your God, who brought you out of Egypt—out of slavery."

Then God gave Moses ten laws for the children of Israel. Some of them told how people should behave toward God; the others told how people should behave toward one another.

You shall have no other gods besides Me, was the first law. Some of the others were: Don't make idols, don't make wrong use of God's name, love your father and mother, don't kill, don't steal, don't tell lies about people, and don't want what doesn't belong to you.

God talked with Moses on the mountaintop many days. He gave Moses two stone tablets with the ten laws carved on them to take back to the children of Israel.

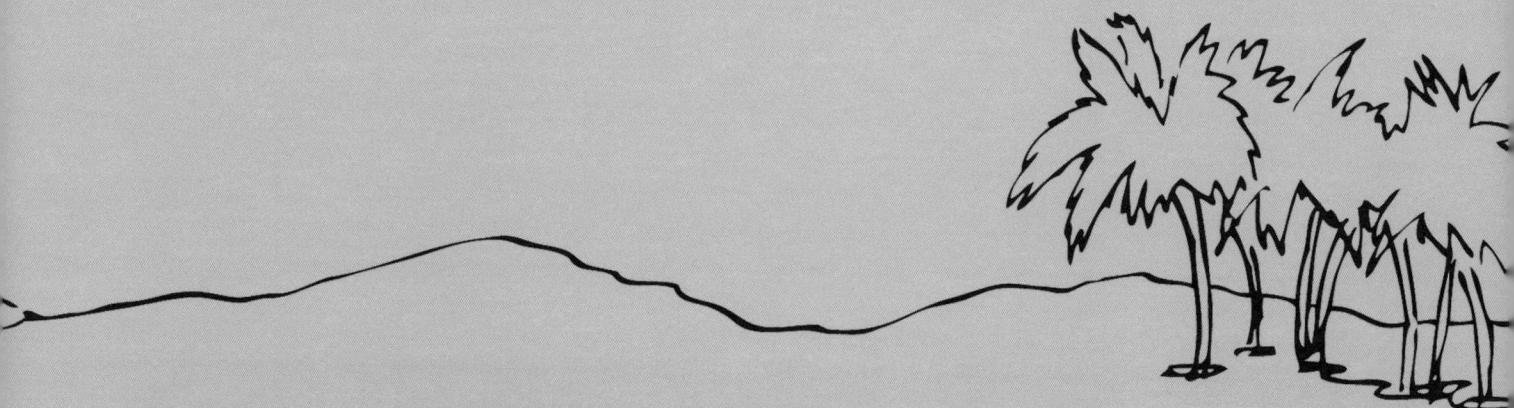

The people in camp were upset because Moses was gone so long. "We don't know what has happened to Moses," they told Aaron. "You must make a god to lead us now."

They gave Aaron their gold jewelry, and he made a golden calf out of it for them to worship instead of worshipping God.

When Moses returned and saw them worshipping the golden calf, he was so angry that they weren't following God that he smashed the stone tablets he'd brought to them. He destroyed the golden calf, too.

God said to Moses, "Cut two more tablets like those you broke, and go back up to the top of Mount Sinai. I shall give you My laws again."

When Moses came back to the camp this time, even though he had been gone many days, the people were waiting eagerly for him. They took the tablets happily. They made a beautiful box for them and a tent to keep the box in. The tablets reminded them that God was with them.

Listening to God, Moses led them on through the wilderness. Just as when they left Egypt, God sent a pillar of cloud to guide them by day, and a pillar of fire by night.

Finally they reached Kadesh with its springs of fresh water.

"Beyond these hills is the land God promised us," Moses said.

God told Moses to send men to explore the land. He sent Caleb and Joshua and ten others. They returned and said that the land was a wonderful place with plenty of good food. "But its people are big and strong, and its cities are huge and walled."

"We can take that land," Caleb said fearlessly.

"No we can't!" others shouted. "Those men are giants. Just looking at them made us feel like grasshoppers."

Once again the people doubted God and wailed, "Let's choose a leader and go back to Egypt."

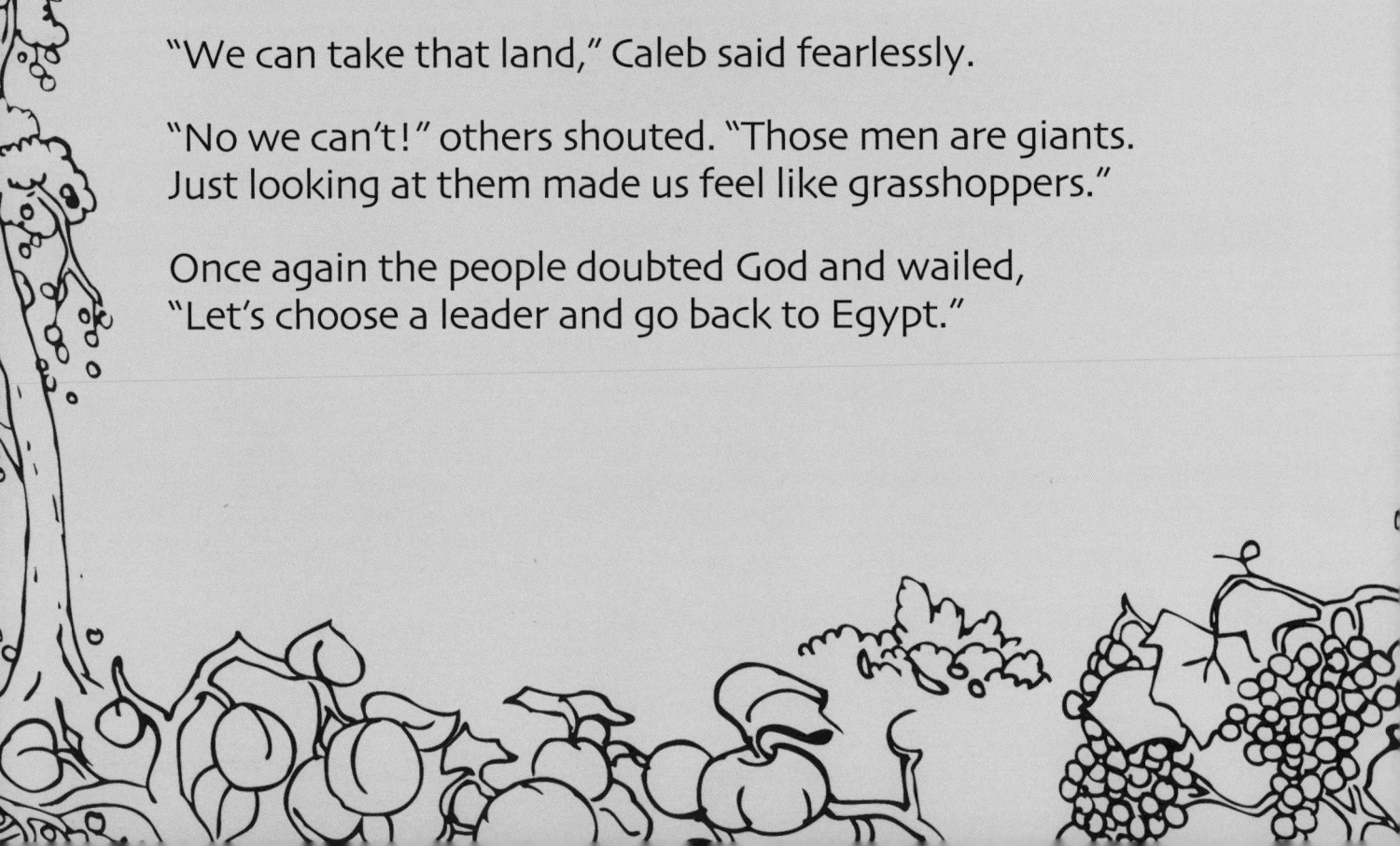

"Listen to us," Caleb and Joshua begged. "The land is good! Trust God. He'll help us."

But the people wouldn't listen. They were still frightened. They returned to the wilderness because they were afraid to follow God.

Moses led them through the wilderness for many weary years. It wasn't an easy journey. Sometimes they traveled far out of the way to avoid enemies. The country they passed through was unfriendly, and sometimes they had to fight hard battles. Finally, they came again to the land God had promised. Only Moses, Caleb, Joshua, and the children of those who came out of Egypt with them were left.

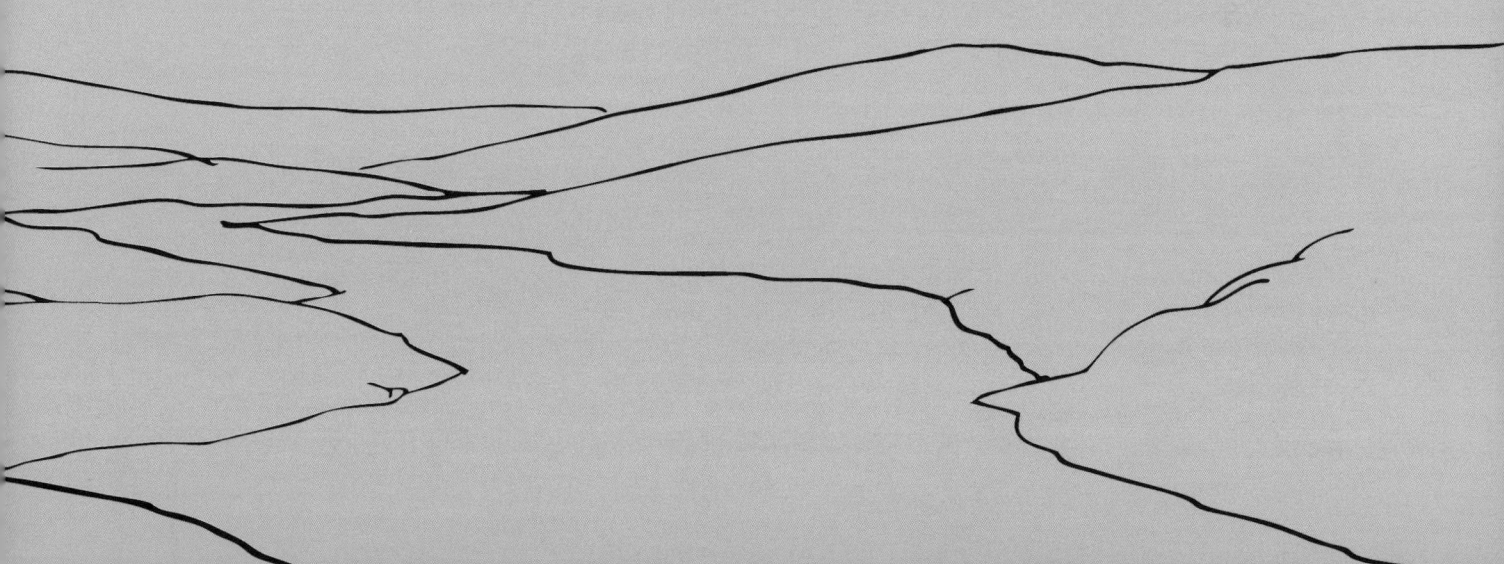

God took Moses to the top of Mount Nebo. "Look," He said. "That good land stretching from the river Jordan to the Great Sea is Canaan, the land I promised to the children of Israel."

So, listening to God, Moses led his people to the land God had promised them. Moses gave them the laws God wanted them to obey—the Ten Commandments.

Moses told the children of Israel, "Tell your children that our people were slaves in Egypt. God brought us out of Egypt into the land He promised us. Also, God told us that loving Him and obeying His laws would bring us great good and keep us happy and safe."

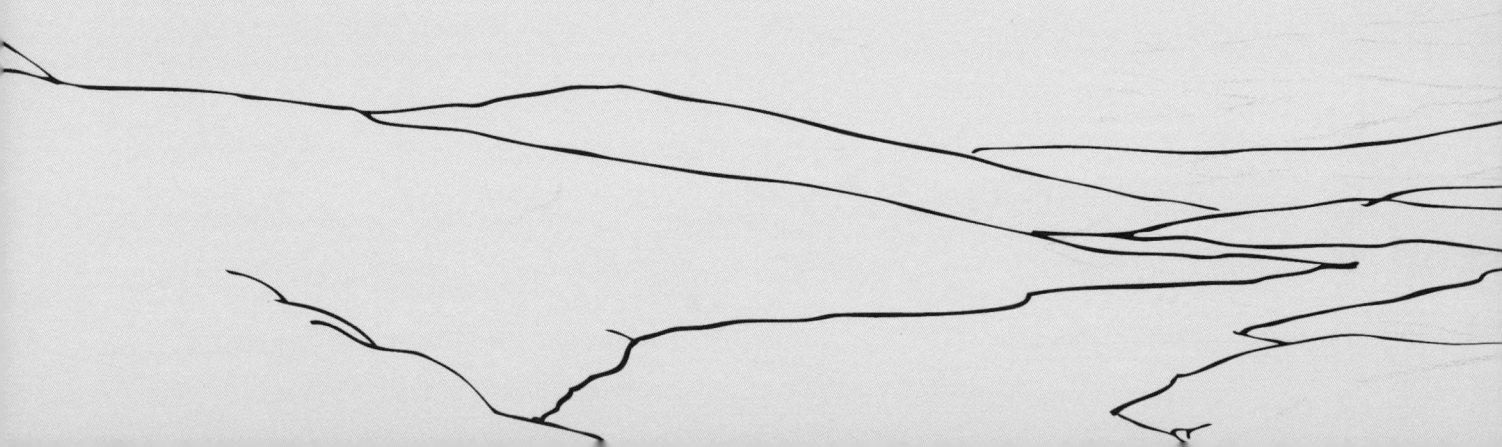

THE TEN COMMANDMENTS

1. Thou shalt have no other gods before me.

2. Thou shalt not make unto thee any graven image, or any likeness of any thing that is in heaven above, or that is in the earth beneath, or that is in the water under the earth: thou shalt not bow down thyself to them, nor serve them: for I the Lord thy God am a jealous God, visiting the iniquity of the fathers upon the children unto the third and fourth generation of them that hate me; and shewing mercy unto thousands of them that love me, and keep my commandments.

3. Thou shalt not take the name of the Lord thy God in vain; for the Lord will not hold him guiltless that taketh his name in vain.

4. Remember the sabbath day, to keep it holy. Six days shalt thou labour, and do all thy work: but the seventh day is the sabbath of the Lord thy God: in it thou shalt not do any work, thou, nor thy son, nor thy daughter, thy manservant, nor thy maidservant, nor thy cattle, nor thy stranger that is within thy gates: for in six days the Lord made heaven and earth, the sea, and all that in them is, and rested the seventh day: wherefore the Lord blessed the sabbath day, and hallowed it.

5. Honour thy father and thy mother: that thy days may be long upon the land which the Lord thy God giveth thee.

6. Thou shalt not kill.

7. Thou shalt not commit adultery.

8. Thou shalt not steal.

9. Thou shalt not bear false witness against thy neighbour.

10. Thou shalt not covet they neighbour's house, thou shalt not covet thy neighbour's wife, nor his manservant, nor his maidservant, nor his ox, nor his ass, nor any thing that is thy neighbour's.

Exodus 20:3-17